Her Bloody Project

poems by

Magdalena Louise Hirt

Finishing Line Press
Georgetown, Kentucky

Her Bloody Project

Copyright © 2025 by Magdalena Louise Hirt
ISBN 979-8-88838-837-2 First Edition
All rights reserved under International and Pan-American Copyright Conventions. No part of this book may be reproduced in any manner whatsoever without written permission from the publisher, except in the case of brief quotations embodied in critical articles and reviews.

ACKNOWLEDGMENTS

I would like to thank my husband for loving and supporting me through the writing of this project and all other endeavors. I love you, Nick.

Publisher: Leah Huete de Maines
Editor: Christen Kincaid
Cover Art: Louis W. Schakel
Author Photo: Nicholas Hirt
Cover Design: Elizabeth Maines McCleavy

Order online: www.finishinglinepress.com
   also available on amazon.com

   Author inquiries and mail orders:
          Finishing Line Press
             PO Box 1626
       Georgetown, Kentucky 40324
                 USA

Contents

The Cover 1

Preface 3

Statements *by the Residents of Culduie* 5

Map *of Deflowered Female Anatomy* 8

The Account of Magdalena Louise Hirt 10

Glossary 21

Medical Reports 23

Extract from *Travels in the Border-Lands of Lunacy* 25

The Trial 28

Epilogue 30

*This poetry is dedicated to Graeme Macrae Burnet
for authorship of His Bloody Project,
to Mandy Haggith's encouragement to dig deeper,
and to my husband & family for loving me and my history*

*Note to Reader
Poetry contains spoilers for the novel His Bloody Project
by Graeme Macrae Burnet*

The Cover

His Bloody Project

The bloody fingerprints lie on my coffee table,
the title and image repelling my children,
and their grandmother—I pick up the book again.
These documents pertaining to a triple murder
are within arm's reach of the inhabitants in our cottage
—untouched due to the fingerprints it contains.
Why does his project, his work, his life, have to be bloody?
Why without opening the pages do I sympathize
with what his motives and circumstance might be?
The leaves turn blood red and fall from the trees
outside my window. I cozy up to the fireplace
and wrap a bearskin looking blanket around me.
Do I heed the warning of "crime" and prepare
to have to submit to unspeakable, but written,
circumstance? Will I trust this narrator who leads
me through the journey? I spread apart the pages
in my fingers noticing sections that will prove
a murderer innocent or guilty—different voices
that will protect or blame these bloody prints.
I become his project—a reader whose mind bends
to defend Roderick Macrae, Roddy, my intellectual
friend that admits to everything. I step into his cell
and hold his hand as he speaks to me—a bucket
of his filth in the corner does not sway me or disgust
me, but tightens my grip on his bloody fingers,
his dirty hands. I slide my fingertips over his
on the smooth cover. My fingers are larger
than his. Will this give me any influence over
what will happen to him. The windows of the croft
homes are filled with darkness that spills
the untold stories within. I read the Highland proverb:
The quern performs best when the grindstone
has been pitted—and before I even start
reading the accounts and documents presented,
I feel like a well-oiled machine already entranced
and believing the narrative as fact. Fingerprints
don't lie and mine gently flip *his* papers, my scars
making me strong enough to turn the pages.

Preface

Moments Collide

The moments collide after reading this.
The task it will make me confront within
myself. My insides bruise exposing blood
on the surface of my delicate skin. I am
scared. Relive. Revive. Battle. Memories.
That is the assignment. My chosen project.
My nails scratch at the hardened scab
I formally thought nonexistent. It bleeds.
Blood trickles down my leg as a decided
river leaving stain on me. I kill a mosquito
that approaches. No more blood to share.

Statements *by the Residents of Culduie*

night creeps in

I've been narratively tricked.

The true crime was hiding under pretty skirts
overlooked by the men of the court, but showing

with bruises—the woman's body, the pull
that pushes men to leave sanity behind,

the pull that gives them permission to take
me as their own, with no consent—raped.

The twist of the end turns my stomach.
Should I blame Graeme Macrae Burnet?

Roderick Macrae? Lachlan Broad? Surely
someone is to blame. Not me. Not me.

Not Flora. Not Jetta. Not me. Not me.

_my_ daughter asks _me_
    ~what kind of friends I had? who were the witnesses?

I've been crying telling
my story of rape to *my*
daughter. She holds *my*
hand. *You* are not a victim.
You are not at fault, she says.

I cringe *my* eyes tightly as *I* can trying to imagine
a story for *her* that doesn't involve so much pain.

What about *your* friends?

I cringe *my* eyes tighter in pain—*my* heart breaking to spill the words:
They were the worst of it, *my* two "best friends," didn't   believe   me.

The morning after, *I* told *them* as *I* watched *them* eat soggy cereal,
its pops and crinkles—changing *my* life forever   in   warm   milk.

A month later. My period was late. *Him—with one of my "friends"—*
watching. One line. Negative. *Them*—running upstairs to celebrate.
Make out.

I fold into *myself*—my chest caves into my stomach like magnets—
imploding, disappearing, *witness* to only *myself* blocked by *myself*

for years—in drugs, with a face and body not my own, *me*—a casing

for dark matter. It made *me* stronger, *I* say to *her*. *I* could recognize
predators with tender smiles offering a "safe" walk home. *I changed.*

There was *dragon* in *my* blood that could start *fires* quickly. *I* squeeze
her hand, know that *my* eyes
are truly *my* eyes when *I* stare
back
at *hers*.

Map *of Deflowered Female Anatomy*

Photo by Louis William Schakel

The Account of
Magdalena Louise Hirt

literary crime

had me grip the table like Jetta
    as Graeme slowly dropped his
        words and left his structure
            "protruding from his breeches"
    there   here
my knuckles sore
    splinters in my skin   a hand strokes my hair
no skirt will cover the bruises in my eyes

        "a puppet whose strings had been cut"

youth   snipped

    "soft outer parts…pulverised"

the sheep in the peat bog
            chokes on blood and bone
my history taken in a single thrill

        the crow blinks
           and stares at me
              turns its head

my sea-ware stripped   soul exposed

    my green floats away   on the surface

        red and brown remains

    no song will return it

fish	**&**	**vulture**
My life has started again	flowing with ebb	lost in travel
The past needs picking	a cleaning	an undoing
I bob on the water	pecking	at plastic keys
Fingers like a beak	breathing	underwater
There it was	rape	that held me under
There it was	poetry	that set me free
The waterbed needed	a pecking	a tear, to bleed
Truth. The vast feathers	needed	a swoop of terror
Upon my past. Above	the water	to make an ocean
I stare at the text	on my screen	mountains out my hatches
I swim back to	confront	you
Your meat	needs	eating
You	are	nothing
You	are only	what I allow you to be
I tear	swallow	spit you out
The moment you	took	from me
Is left behind	in	murk
I	am	the fish
I	am	the vulture
Y	o	u
A	r	e
Meat	and	excrement
A devil sent to destroy	what	it had so little power to touch
My beak tears down	on bone	on hide and muscle
And I throw pieces	to my other	self
I am	well	fed

in the rain

through the bimini
mast anchor lights glow
—orbs, calling stars
and I
am far away
from my
past

how do I put the past
parallel to where I am

now

the literature haunts me
a project that claims me
swirls in my blood, there

I see *him*

like it was yesterday
wrestling with me
my arms, my legs
a fluid wrestle
on a waterbed
in the dark
an hour-long
struggle

Here

On my waterbed—My Sailboat
I Am Sturdy

I Am
Not
Wrestled

I Am Free.

Parallel apparent?
Parallel lost?

Fact with fact

The only fiction
His Bloody Project

A Tree

A tree began to grow in me
strong oak, evergreen pine,
sweeping weeping willow.
It was a tree that straightened
my spine, aided in my ability
to look others in the eyes.
My boughs stretched over
the girls at my college,
my dorm cluster girls.
Men—were not welcome
under the tree or sauntering
the grounds of our soil.
I was in control of nesting.
I am a tree with no name,
no need for definition.
I hold my own water,
oxygen, mixing breeds,
adapting to protect,
to recognize the wood-
cutter. The ones I love
grow like ivy feeding
safely what I protect
and provide, protect,
protect, protect. At night,
my leaves glow vibrant
dancing in the wind
making homes for trauma
fostering the damaged
into flowers. Adapt,
adopt, adept with my own
formation of night—
no woman-girl of mine
need to fear the darkness—
only feed on mystery
of my roots that give
them a strong ground
to photosynthesize—
hybrids of femininity.

Soft Lips
~Flora's love for Ishbel

There was exhibition—
    two girls kissing for show.
Times where I kissed you—
    for show. It. Was never.
For them. It was always—
    For me. The softest lips
I ever touched—deepest,
    tender eyes that looked
at me—in return, lost, I was—
    in wild hair, your mind, music.

There was a moment
    I allowed myself
        to do what I wanted.
There was you. So many of them—
    but always you. Why not you?
Why search for one of them?
    Keep one of them? Be with—
…one of them—the hands, love,
    and holding was only found in you.
You, with small hands, searching eyes—
    ready to please lips—no disguise. Me. You.
Lingering there. I was swimming to the surface.

The Sea-ware

was to your father like Flora's skirt
was to you. There for the taking,
a woman, like the sea, thought
she was free to sing—keep you
company. Like your father, you
had to take what wasn't yours
to fertilize your needs. Perhaps
the green gloss of the ocean
should have clung to the rocks.
Perhaps the melody of woman-
hood should have clung to Flora's
legs, her skin, her innocence. Sea-
ware like freedom grows, spreads
within deceiving. Like the sea-ware,
freedom needs to cling to part
of the soul. When broken, breaks
free to ride wave, wind—leaving
a rock bare for taking. Perhaps,
Roddy, you should have listened
to your teacher, left to leave
never possessing altering sea,
song, legs, land, freedom, or her.

Grasping Grass with Fists

7
On the grass, in roots, Roddy's fists
were predetermined with potential.
Even a woman, of your past soil, time,
Flora, had plans to do, to move, grow.

You struck her down, reaping, to keep
her to the land, dig her in dirt, that you
could not escape. Fines and money
taken for your cock crowing in the dark.

6
They split your land, sections, to keep,
you poor. Ruined your potential harvest
by prohibiting sea-ware, fertilization,
stagnation, it became barren, desolate.

Your father stopped smoking, singing.
They raped your sister. Leaving seeds
inside her, their property. Stains.
Constable. Laird. Forever present.

5
Were they raping your mother?
Keeping her to the land, used.
Did they send the crows to watch?
Did you tend to them, unknowingly?

Then, you finally noticed Flora, woman,
sweeping the land, you were rooted, tied.
A stare game, in innocence, bound her.
Milk served, a symbol, misinterpreted.

4
Her body was singing of freedom
that you had to ruin. Your thoughts

were no longer of father's injustice.
Sight of song, made you stalk night.

Doing nothing with your life, teasing
crows with mice, she called the devil
to find work for your idle hands. Eggs,
she put in them, and a walk she gave.

3
You made her laugh, so your father
forbade it, like land forbade you to leave.
In darkness, you wished nightgowns,
candlelight, unobserved windows.

Invisible regulations. No future. You
longed to see Flora. She became
your escape, your reason, your
ownership. No permission granted.

2
Finding her on the dyke, she
accompanied you to nowhere.
Here, you married her, in your
mind, walking land, neither owned.

The devil took your tongue. The old
crone saw you. Culduie grasped you.
Your doorstep was the laird's, your
stones in the wall were Lachlan's.

1
Nothing belonged to you, so you
chose to take, Flora, the flower, you
a stem. Her petals wind spread
were grasped, crushed with thrust.

Like the shawl Jetta made forced
into thorns, you were taught cock

in a henhouse, proclaimed feelings
that were slapped away by the moss.

0
You should have kept walking, but land,
your place, your people pulled. Tethered,
a flaughter and cock became your
weapon. You pulverized what you could.

Flora was of sea-ware, barn doors, nests,
moments in movement, song, coastlines.
You became what you hated, the fence,
burnt peat, criminal, rapist, brutality, laird.

Glossary

a poem entered

at sixteen

                        waterbed

in a basement

                        friend of a friend

stares

soggy cheerios

                        denial

no support

                        secrets that bled

my virginity

                only a poem could replace

Medical Reports

My Statistics

One in three
female victims
of completed
or attempted
rape
experienced it
for the first time
between the ages
of 11 and 17.
About half (51.1%)
of female victims
of rape
reported being raped
by an intimate partner
and 40.8%
by an acquaintance.

Found poem statistics from: https://www.nsvrc.org/statistics
National Sexual Violence Resource Center

Extract from
Travels in the Border-Lands of Lunacy

"border-lands of lunacy"

a psychiatrist picks up his pen
makes a judgement
bites the end, ink stains
his lip, blame—the father

two gentlemen approach Culduie
a good intention, a scientific one
ripe with judgements, the father
steals for his pipe, alone now

hung pregnant daughter, murderer
for a son, three children taken
for better circumstance, but he,
under Freud, under dreams, dwells

in dirt, Roderick Macrae, beaten
into submission, refuses wine
in his cell—too rich—gentrified,
keep the cork from the filth bucket

that remains in the corner, like skull
fragments in Flora's brain matter,
her dad deserved something awful,
does Roddy's father's calloused hands?

Was the "prisoner speaking to himself"?

Aren't we all doing this
          all the time
in our vast imaginary
                    minds?

What does it matter
if our mouths move
a bit   as we do so, —or
some of what we think
mutters to the tips   of our lips
                                    —silent speak?

"He would cease...muttering"
—no one would know his thoughts?
Privacy. Movement. Passion?

Freud speaks, the "public self is a conditioned construct
of the inner psychological self"—Expression?

more so

than the
conditioned,
social-norm
pressured

I ask my husband and son to stop talking to me—I need

to concentrate—at this point, have I forgotten how—without social
construction? Am I completely worked over by eyes
that glare, roll, or demean

Me.   constable   stranger

Do I give power away?   to plead

The Trial

Embracing Evil
~an ethical poem for Roderick

You'd been wronged. I embraced you
ignoring the clues, making excuses. I

didn't see it coming. You stalked the night,
but in the day showed me delicacy. I

searched you out for company, but I
never led you on. I told you no. I

aggressively reacted to you, but still,
it was complex, your father, my father

opposing each other set us to be Juliet
and Romeo. That bird in the barn didn't

live or fly away. Your sister hung broken,
a different kind of victim, motherless

like the bird. I would have taken the rope,
the stool, her hand and led her out. I

would have seen, so why did I hope
for you till the end when it was obvious?

Blindfolded. I was captured with story.
Time involved in tale. Perhaps I

would have taken your hand, and led
you away. Forgiveness is complicated.

Epilogue

Guilty

You
Cannot plead insanity. You
Are Guilty of taking advantage. You
Are Guilty of being older. You
Are Guilty of lack of control. You
Are Guilty of not being a gentleman. You
Are Guilty of stronger arms. You
Are Guilty of stronger legs. You
Are Guilty of taking. You
Are Guilty of the night. You
Are Guilty of darkness. You
Are Guilty of doing what you want. You
Are Guilty of moving on. You
Are Guilty of lies. You
Are Guilty of walking with me. You
Are Guilty of admiring me. You
Are Guilty of telling me nice things. You
Are Guilty of at first being gentle. You
Are Guilty of biding your time. You
Are Guilty of letting it get late. You
Are Guilty of wanting to be alone with me. You
Are Guilty of your intentions. You
Are Guilty of not listening to no for hours. You
Are Guilty of overpowering me when tired. You
Are Guilty of my limp body. You
Are Guilty of taking my virginity. You
Are Guilty of being 21, me 16. You
Are Guilty of knowing better. You
Are Guilty of stealing my virginity. You
Are Guilty of being a sexual predator. You
Are Guilty of being a rapist. You
Are Guilty of manipulation. You
Are Guilty of motive. You
Are Guilty of moving on. You
Are Guilty of seducing my friends. You
Are Guilty of having what you want. You
Are Guilty of being guilty, and if I could see you

I would feel sorry for your wife, feel sorry for your daughter,
And I would tell the truth that You
Have no power Over ME. I grew, saw, saved. I
Am Not a victim. I
Am Not yours. I
Shared MY STORY that you
Did NOT DeStRoY. I
Am a Survivor Woman Strong. you
are failure loser lost. I
RID MYSELF OF you. you
took what was not yours. you

are small. I AM ME.

For Help, Action, or Support:

- Contact National Health Services (**CNHS**) in the UK https://www.nhs.uk/live-well/sexual-health/help-after-rape-and-sexual-assault/
- Or contact National Sexual Violence Resource Center (**NSVRC**) in the US https://www.nsvrc.org/find-help
- Or **RAINN** (Rape, Abuse & Incest National Network) at rainn.org
    +1.800.656.HOPE (4673)

Or international help:

- **The Handbook of International Centers for Survivors of Sexual Assault and Harassment** https://www.interaction.org/wp-content/uploads/resource-library/international_centers_for_survivors_of_sexual_assault_45553.pdf
- **International Rape Crisis Hotline Directories** http://www.ibiblio.org/rcip/internl.html

Magdalena Louise Hirt has a Master of Arts in English Literature from the University of Toledo and a Master of Letters from the University of Highlands and Islands for Scottish Highlands and Islands Literature.

Magdalena has multiple published articles in *Cruising World*, one in *Enchanted Living*, and another in *Literary Traveler*. Her first four poetry chapbooks, *Levels of the Ocean, Her Sea-filled Arms: Layers of Blue, Pacific Pieces,* and *Pacific Prescription: Leukemia Cyclone* are available for purchase. One more chapbook, *Her Bloody Project*, and her first book, *Distant Story Blue*, are due to be released January of 2025. She has four self-published chapbooks, an article published via E-book from being a featured speaker at a conference in Oxford, and poems that have been published in *The Holland Sentinel, News from Hope College, The Mill* from the University of Toledo, and on display at the Toledo Museum of Art, which included first place and finalist awards. At Grand Valley State University, she received 1st place in fiction and 2nd place in poetry for the Oldenburg Writing Contest. She has been a featured speaker at a literary conference in Boston and two Poetry Speaks at the University of Toledo. She is currently finishing a script, a novel, and another poetry chapbook. With her teaching degree, she has taught Middle School Language Arts and Freshman Composition at the University of Toledo.

Currently, she homeschools her four children and writes from her sailboat, which is a Westerly 49, named Selkie. Their family of six sails to circumnavigate the globe. So far, they have cruised, wintered, and been through lockdown in the following locations: the Great Lakes of Michigan, the Caribbean, the Bahamas, Bermuda, Azores, Ireland, Scotland, Norway, the circle of the Baltic Sea, the Bay of Biscay, Canary Isles, Cape Verde, back to the Caribbean, the Dominican Republic, Guatemala, Panama, French Polynesia, the Kingdom of Tonga, and New Zealand. These locations completed an Atlantic circumnavigation and a Pacific crossing. Her family plans to finish a global circumnavigation by 2027 and continue to sail.

Magdalena enjoys cooking and dancing—most of the time together. With pen, spatula, and helm in hand, her sailing soul belongs on the sea where she chooses words, academics, ingredients, and destinations. Follow their story at www.sealongingselkie.net.

www.ingramcontent.com/pod-product-compliance
Lightning Source LLC
Chambersburg PA
CBHW061031180426
43194CB00036B/170